SHAMBHALA LIBRARY

THE WISDOM
OF THE DESERT

*Sayings from the Desert Fathers
of the Fourth Century*

TRANSLATED BY
Thomas Merton

SHAMBHALA
Boston & London
2004

FRONTISPIECE: Photograph of Thomas Merton by Sybille Akers. Used with permission of the Merton Legacy Trust.

SHAMBHALA PUBLICATIONS, INC.
Horticultural Hall
300 Massachusetts Avenue
Boston, Massachusetts 02115
www.shambhala.com

9 8 7 6 5 4 3 2 1

First Shambhala Library Edition
PRINTED IN CHINA
⊚ This edition is printed on acid-free paper that meets the
American National Standards Institute z39.48 Standard.
Distributed in the United States by Random House, Inc.,
and in Canada by Random House of Canada Ltd

Nihil Obstat: Austin B. Vaughan, S.T.D., Censor Deputatus
Imprimatur: Francis Cardinal Spellman, Archbishop of New York
EX PARTE ORDINIS:
Nihil Obstat: Frater M. Thomas Aquinas Porter, O.C.S.O., Frater
    M. Gabriel O'Connell, O.C.S.O.
Imprimi Potest: Frater M. Gabriel Sortais, O.C.S.O., Abbas Generalis

The Library of Congress catalogues the previous edition
of this book as follows:
Verba seniorum. English. Selections.
The wisdom of the desert/[selected and] translated
[from the Latin] by Thomas Merton.
p.   cm.
Originally published: New Directions, 1970.
ISBN 0-87773-976-5 (Shambhala Pocket Classics)
ISBN 1-59030-039-4 (Shambhala Library)
1. Spiritual life—Christianity—Quotations, maxims, etc.
2. Monastic and religious life—Quotations, maxims, etc.
3. Desert Fathers—Quotations.   I. Merton, Thomas, 1915-1968.
BR63.V4132   1994   93-23927   271'.009'015—dc20   CIP

CONTENTS

AUTHOR'S NOTE

THIS COLLECTION of sayings from the *Verba Seniorum* is by no means intended as a piece of research scholarship. It is, on the contrary, a free and informal redaction of stories chosen here and there in the various original Latin versions, without order and without any identification of the particular sources. The book is designed entirely for the reader's interest and edification. In other words I have felt that as a monk of the twentieth century I ought to be quite free in availing myself of the privilege enjoyed by the monks of earlier days, and so I have made a little collection of my own, with no special system, order or purpose, merely in order to have the stories and to enjoy them with my friends. This is the way such books originally came into existence.

When the first version of this work was completed, I gave it to my friend Victor Hammer who printed an extraordinarily beautiful limited edition on his hand press in Lexington, Kentucky. After that, it was decided to expand the collection a little, and rewrite the introduction, so that New Directions could bring out a larger edition. So here it is. But I hope the book still preserves its original spontaneous, informal and personal aspect. Far from detracting from their wisdom, this informality will guarantee the stories the authenticity they have always had and keep them fresh and alive in all their concreteness and immediacy. May those who need and enjoy such apothegms be encouraged, by the taste of clear water, to follow the brook to its source.

The Wisdom
of the Desert

The Wisdom of the Desert

I N THE FOURTH CENTURY A.D. the deserts of
Egypt, Palestine, Arabia and Persia were peopled by a race of men who have left behind them a
strange reputation. They were the first Christian
hermits, who abandoned the cities of the pagan
world to live in solitude. Why did they do this? The
reasons were many and various, but they can all be
summed up in one word as the quest for "salvation." And what was salvation? Certainly it was not
something they sought in mere exterior conformity
to the customs and dictates of any social group. In
those days men had become keenly conscious of
the strictly individual character of "salvation." Society—which meant pagan society, limited by the
horizons and prospects of life "in this world"—was
regarded by them as a shipwreck from which each
single individual man had to swim for his life. We
need not stop here to discuss the fairness of this
view: what matters is to remember that it was a
fact. These were men who believed that to let oneself drift along, passively accepting the tenets and

values of what they knew as society, was purely and simply a disaster. The fact that the Emperor was now Christian and that the "world" was coming to know the Cross as a sign of temporal power only strengthened them in their resolve.

It should seem to us much stranger than it does, this paradoxical flight from the world that attained its greatest dimensions (I almost said frenzy) when the "world" became officially Christian. These men seem to have thought, as a few rare modern thinkers like Berdyaev have thought, that there is really no such thing as a "Christian state." They seem to have doubted that Christianity and politics could ever be mixed to such an extent as to produce a fully Christian society. In other words, for them the only Christian society was spiritual and extramundane: the Mystical Body of Christ. These were surely extreme views, and it is almost scandalous to recall them in a time like ours when Christianity is accused on all sides of preaching negativism and withdrawal—of having no effective way of meeting the problems of the age. But let us not be too superficial. The Desert Fathers did, in fact, meet the "problems of their time" in the sense that *they* were among the few who were ahead of their time, and opened the way for the development of a new man and a new society. They represent what modern social philosophers (Jaspers, Mumford) call the emergence of the "axial man," the forerunner of the modern person- alist man. The eighteenth and nineteenth cen- turies with their pragmatic individualism degraded and corrupted the psychological heritage of axial man with its debt to the Desert Fathers and other contemplatives, and prepared the way for the great regression to the herd mentality that is taking place now.

The flight of these men to the desert was nei- ther purely negative nor purely individualistic. They were not rebels against society. True, they were in a certain sense "anarchists," and it will do no harm to think of them in that light. They were men who did not believe in letting themselves be passively guided and ruled by a decadent state, and who believed that there was a way of getting along without slavish dependence on accepted, conventional values. But they did not intend to place themselves above society. They did not re- ject society with proud contempt, as if they were superior to other men. On the contrary, one of the reasons why they fled from the world of men was that in the world men were divided into those who were successful, and imposed their will on others, and those who had to give in and be imposed upon. The Desert Fathers declined to be ruled by men, but had no desire to rule over others themselves. Nor did they fly from human fellowship—the very fact that they uttered these "words" of advice to one another is proof that they were eminently social. The society they sought was one where all men were truly equal, where the only authority under God was the charismatic authority of wisdom, experience and love. Of course, they acknowledged the benevolent, hierarchical authority of their bishops: but the bishops were far away and said little about what went on in the desert until the great Origenist conflict at the end of the fourth century.

What the Fathers sought most of all was their own true self, in Christ. And in order to do this, they had to reject completely the false, formal self, fabricated under social compulsion in "the world." They sought a way to God that was uncharted and freely chosen, not inherited from others who had mapped it out beforehand. They sought a God whom they alone could find, not one who was "given" in a set, stereotyped form by somebody else. Not that they rejected any of the dogmatic formulas of the Christian faith: they accepted and clung to them in their simplest and most elementary shape. But they were slow (at least in the beginning, in the time of their primitive wisdom) to get involved in theological controversy. Their flight to the arid horizons of the desert meant also a refusal to be content with arguments, concepts and technical verbiage.

We deal here exclusively with hermits. There were also cenobites in the desert—cenobites by the hundred and by the thousand, living the "common life" in enormous monasteries like the one founded by St. Pachomius at Tabenna. Among these there was social order, almost military discipline. Nevertheless the spirit was still very much a spirit of personalism and freedom, because even the cenobite knew that his Rule was only an exterior framework, a kind of scaffolding with which he was to help himself build the spiritual structure of his own life with God. But the hermits were in every way more free. There was nothing to which they had to "conform" except the secret, hidden, inscrutable will of God which might differ very notably from one cell to another! It is very significant that one of the first of these *Verba* (Number 3) is one in which the authority of St. Anthony is adduced for what is the basic principle of desert life: that God is the authority and that apart from His manifest will there are few or no principles: "Therefore, whatever you see your soul to desire according to God, do that thing, and you shall keep your heart safe."

Obviously such a path could only be travelled by one who was very alert and very sensitive to the landmarks of a trackless wilderness. The hermit had to be a man mature in faith, humble and detached from himself to a degree that is altogether terrible. The spiritual cataclysms that sometimes overtook some of the presumptuous visionaries of the desert are there to show the dangers of the lonely life—like bones whitening in the sand. The Desert Father could not afford to be an illuminist. He could not dare risk attachment to his own ego, or the dangerous ecstasy of self-will. He could not retain the slightest identification with his superficial, transient, self-constructed self. He had to lose himself in the inner, hidden reality of a self that was transcendent, mysterious, half-known, and lost in Christ. He had to die to the values of transient existence as Christ had died to them on the Cross, and rise from the dead with Him in the light of an entirely new wisdom. Hence the life of sacrifice, which started out from a clean break, separating the monk from the world. A life continued in "compunction" which taught him to lament the madness of attachment to unreal values. A life of solitude and labour, poverty and fasting, charity and prayer which enabled the old superficial self to be purged away and permitted the gradual emergence of the true, secret self in which the Believer and Christ were "one Spirit."

Finally, the proximate end of all this striving was "purity of heart"—a clear unobstructed vision of the true state of affairs, an intuitive grasp of one's own inner reality as anchored, or rather lost, in God through Christ. The fruit of this was *quies*: "rest." Not rest of the body, nor even fixation of the exalted spirit upon some point or summit of light. The Desert Fathers were not, for the most part, ecstatics. Those who were have left some strange and misleading stories behind them to confuse the true issue. The "rest" which these men sought was simply the sanity and poise of a being that no longer has to look at itself because it is carried away by the perfection of freedom that is in it. And carried where? Wherever Love itself, or the Divine Spirit, sees fit to go. Rest, then, was a kind of simple nowhereness and no-mindedness that had lost all preoccupation with a false or limited "self." At peace in the possession of a sublime "Nothing" the spirit laid hold, in secret, upon the "All"—without trying to know what it possessed.

Now the Fathers were not even sufficiently concerned with the nature of this rest to speak of it in these terms, except very rarely, as did St. Anthony, when he remarked that "the prayer of the monk is not perfect until he no longer realizes himself or the fact that he is praying." And this was said casually, in passing. For the rest, the Fathers steered clear of everything lofty, everything esoteric, everything theoretical or difficult to understand. That is to say, they refused to talk about such things. And for that matter they were not very willing to talk about anything else, even about the truths of Christian faith, which accounts for the laconic quality of these sayings.

In many respects, therefore, these Desert Fathers had much in common with Indian Yogis and with Zen Buddhist monks of China and Japan. If we were to seek their like in twentieth-century America, we would have to look in strange, out of the way places. Such beings are tragically rare. They obviously do not flourish on the sidewalk at Forty-Second Street and Broadway. We might perhaps find someone like this among the Pueblo Indians or the Navahos: but there the case would be entirely different. You would have simplicity, primitive wisdom: but rooted in a primitive society. With the Desert Fathers, you have the characteristic of a clean break with a conventional, accepted social context in order to swim for one's life into an apparently irrational void.

Though I might be expected to claim that men like this could be found in some of our monasteries of contemplatives, I will not be so bold. With us it is often rather a case of men leaving the society of the "world" in order to fit themselves into another kind of society, that of the religious family which they enter. They exchange the values, concepts and rites of the one for those of the other. And since we now have centuries of monasticism behind us, this puts the whole thing in a different light. The social "norms" of a monastic family are also apt to be conventional, and to live by them does not involve a leap into the void—only a radical change of customs and standards. The words and examples of the Desert Fathers have been so much a part of monastic tradition that time has turned them into stereotypes for us, and we are no longer able to notice their fabulous originality. We have buried them, so to speak, in our own routines, and thus securely insulated ourselves against any form of spiritual shock from their lack of conventionality. Yet it has been my hope that in selecting and editing these "words" I may have presented them in a new light and made their freshness once again obvious.

The Desert Fathers were pioneers, with nothing to go on but the example of some of the prophets, like St. John the Baptist, Elias, Eliseus, and the Apostles, who also served them as models. For the rest, the life they embraced was "angelic" and they walked the untrodden paths of invisible spirits. Their cells were the furnace of Babylon in which, in the midst of flames, they found themselves with Christ.

They neither courted the approval of their contemporaries nor sought to provoke their disapproval, because the opinions of others had ceased, for them, to be matters of importance. They had no set doctrine about freedom, but they had in fact become free by paying the price of freedom.

In any case these Fathers distilled for themselves a very practical and unassuming wisdom that is at once primitive and timeless, and which enables us to reopen the sources that have been polluted or blocked up altogether by the accumulated mental and spiritual refuse of our technological barbarism. Our time is in desperate need of this kind of simplicity. It needs to recapture something of the experience reflected in these lines. The word to emphasize is *experience*. The few short phrases collected in this volume have little or no value merely as information. It would be futile to skip through these pages and lightly take note of the fact that the Fathers said this and this. What good will it do us to know merely that such things were once *said?* The important thing is that they were lived. That they flow from an experience of the deeper levels of life. That they represent a discovery of man, at the term of an inner and spiritual journey that is far more crucial and infinitely more important than any journey to the moon.

What can we gain by sailing to the moon if we are not able to cross the abyss that separates us from ourselves? This is the most important of all voyages of discovery, and without it all the rest are not only useless but disastrous. Proof: the great travellers and colonizers of the Renaissance were, for the most part, men who perhaps were capable of the things they did precisely because they were alienated from themselves. In the subjugating primitive worlds they only imposed on them, with the force of cannons, their own confusion and their own alienation. Superb exceptions like Fray Bartholome de las Casas, St. Francis Xavier, or Father Matthew Ricci, only prove the rule.

These sayings of the Desert Fathers are drawn from a classical collection, the *Verba Seniorum,* in Migne's *Latin Patrology* (Volume 73). The *Verba* are distinguished from the other Desert Fathers' literature by their total lack of literary artifice, their complete and honest simplicity. The *Lives* of the Fathers are much more grandiloquent, dramatic, stylized. They abound in wonderful events and in miracles. They are strongly marked by the literary personalities to whom we owe them. But the *Verba* are the plain, unpretentious reports that went from mouth to mouth in the Coptic tradition before being committed to writing in Syriac, Greek and Latin.

Always simple and concrete, always appealing to the experience of the man who had been shaped by solitude, these proverbs and tales were intended as plain answers to plain questions. Those who came to the desert seeking "salvation" asked the elders for a "word" that would help them to find it—a *verbum salutis,* a "word of salvation." The answers were not intended to be general, universal prescriptions. Rather they were originally concrete and precise keys to particular doors that had to be entered, at a given time, by given individuals. Only later, after much repetition and much quotation, did they come to be regarded as common currency. It will help us to understand these sayings better if we remember their practical and, one might say, existential quality. But by the time St. Benedict in his Rule prescribed that the "Words of the Fathers" were to be read aloud frequently before Compline, they were traditional monastic lore.

The Fathers were humble and silent men, and did not have much to say. They replied to questions in few words, to the point. Rather than give an abstract principle, they preferred to tell a concrete story. Their brevity is refreshing, and rich in content. There is more light and satisfaction in these laconic sayings than in many a long ascetic treatise full of details about ascending from one "degree" to another in the spiritual life. These words of the Fathers are never theoretical in our modern sense of the word. They are never abstract. They deal with concrete things and with jobs to be done in the everyday life of a fourth-century monk. But what is said serves just as well for a twentieth-century thinker. The basic realities of the interior life are there: faith, humility, charity, meekness, discretion, self-denial. But not the least of the qualities of the "words of salvation" is their common sense.

This is important. The Desert Fathers later acquired a reputation for fanaticism because of the stories that were told about their ascetic feats by indiscreet admirers. They were indeed ascetics: but when we read their own words and see what they themselves thought about life, we find that they were anything but fanatics. They were humble, quiet, sensible people, with a deep knowledge of human nature and enough understanding of the things of God to realize that they knew very little about Him. Hence they were not much disposed to make long speeches about the divine essence, or even to declaim on the mystical meaning of Scripture. If these men say little about God, it is because they know that when one has been somewhere close to His dwelling, silence makes more sense than a lot of words. The fact that Egypt, in their time, was seething with religious and intellectual controversies was all the more reason for them to keep their mouths shut. There were the Neo-Platonists, the Gnostics, the

Stoics and Pythagoreans. There were the various, highly vocal, orthodox and heretical groups of Christians. There were the Arians (whom the monks of the Desert passionately resisted). There were the Origenists (and some of the monks were faithfully devoted followers of Origen). In all this noise, the desert had no contribution to offer but a discreet and detached silence.

The great monastic centres of the fourth century were in Egypt, Arabia and Palestine. Most of these stories concern hermits of Nitria and Scete, in northern Egypt, near the Mediterranean coast and west of the Nile. There were also many colonies of monks in the Nile Delta. The Thebaid, near ancient Thebes, further inland along the Nile, was another centre of monastic activity, particularly of the cenobites. Palestine had early attracted monks from all parts of the Christian world, the most famous of them being St. Jerome, who lived and translated the Scriptures in a cave at Bethlehem. Then there was an important monastic colony around Mount Sinai in Arabia: founders of that monastery of St. Catherine which has recently broken into the news with the "discovery" of the works of Byzantine art preserved there.

What kind of life did the Fathers lead? A word of

explanation may help us understand their sayings better. The Desert Fathers are usually referred to as "Abbot" (*abbas*) or "Elder" (*senex*). An Abbot was not then, as now, a canonically elected superior of a community, but any monk or hermit who had been tried by years in the desert and proved himself a servant of God. With them, or near them, lived "Brethren" and "Novices"—those who were still in the process of learning the life. The novices still needed the continuous supervision of an elder, and lived with one in order to be instructed by his word and example. The brethren lived on their own, but occasionally resorted to a nearby elder for advice.

Most of the characters represented in these sayings and stories are men who are "on the way" to purity of heart rather than men who have fully arrived. The Desert Fathers, inspired by Clement and Origen, and the Neo-Platonic tradition, were sometimes confident that they could rise above all passion and become impervious to anger, lust, pride and all the rest. But we find little in these sayings to encourage those who believed that Christian perfection was a matter of *apatheia* (impassivity). The praise of monks "beyond all passion" seems indeed to have come from tourists who passed briefly through the deserts and went home to write books about what they had seen, rather than from those who had spent their whole life in the wilderness. These latter were much more inclined to accept the common realities of life and be content with the ordinary lot of man who has to struggle all his life to overcome himself. The wisdom of the *Verba* is seen in the story of the monk John, who boasted that he was "beyond all temptation" and was advised by a shrewd elder to pray to God for a few good solid battles in order that his life might continue to be worth something.

At certain times, all the solitaries and novices would come together for the liturgical *synaxis* (Mass and prayers in common) and after this they might eat together and hold a kind of chapter meeting to discuss communal problems. Then they returned to their solitude, where they spent their time working and praying.

They supported themselves by the labour of their hands, usually weaving baskets and mats out of palm leaves or reeds. These they sold in the nearby towns. There is sometimes question in the *Verba* of matters relating to the work and to the commerce involved. Charity and hospitality were matters of top priority, and took precedence over fasting and personal ascetic routines. The countless sayings which bear witness to this warmhearted friendliness should be sufficient to take care of accusations that these men hated their own kind. Indeed there was more real love, understanding and kindliness in the desert than in the cities, where, then as now, it was every man for himself.

This fact is all the more important because the very essence of the Christian message is charity, unity in Christ. The Christian mystics of all ages sought and found not only the unification of their own being, not only union with God, but union with one another in the Spirit of God. To seek a union with God that would imply complete separation, in spirit as well as in body from all the rest of mankind, would be to a Christian saint not only absurd but the very opposite of sanctity. Isolation in the self, inability to go out of oneself to others, would mean incapacity for any form of self-transcendence. To be thus the prisoner of one's own selfhoood is, in fact, to be in hell: a truth that Sartre, though professing himself an atheist, has expressed in the most arresting fashion in his play *No Exit (Huis Clos)*.

All through the *Verba Seniorum* we find a repeated insistence on the primacy of love over everything else in the spiritual life: over knowledge, gnosis, asceticism, contemplation, solitude, prayer. Love in fact *is* the spiritual life, and without it all the other exercises of the spirit, however lofty, are emptied of content and become mere illusions. The more lofty they are, the more dangerous the illusion.

Love, of course, means something much more that mere sentiment, much more than token favours and perfunctory almsdeeds. Love means an interior and spiritual identification with one's brother, so that he is not regarded as an "object" to "which" one "does good." The fact is that good done to another as to an object is of little or no spiritual value. Love takes one's neighbour as one's other self, and loves him with all the immense humility and discretion and reserve and reverence without which no one can presume to enter into the sanctuary of another's subjectivity. From such love all authoritarian brutality, all exploitation, domineering and condescension must necessarily be absent. The saints of the desert were enemies of every subtle or gross expedient by which "the spiritual man" contrives to bully those he thinks inferior to him-

self, thus gratifying his own ego. They had re-
nounced everything that savoured of punishment
and revenge, however hidden it might be.

The charity of the Desert Fathers is not set before us in unconvincing effusions. The full diffi-
culty and magnitude of the task of loving others is
recognized everywhere and never minimized. It is
hard to really love others if love is to be taken in
the full sense of the word. Love demands a complete inner transformation—for without this we
cannot possibly come to identify ourselves with
our brother. We have to become, in some sense,
the person we love. And this involves a kind of
death of our own being, our own self. No matter
how hard we try, we resist this death: we fight
back with anger, with recriminations, with demands, with ultimatums. We seek any convenient
excuse to break off and give up the difficult task.
But in these *Verba Seniorum* we read of Abbot
Ammonas, who spent fourteen years praying to
overcome anger, or rather, more significantly, to
be delivered from it. We read of Abbot Serapion,
who sold his last book, a copy of the Gospels, and
gave the money to the poor, thus selling "the very
words which told him to sell all and give to the
poor." Another Abbot severely rebuked some

monks who had caused a group of robbers to be thrown in jail, and as a result the shame-faced hermits broke into the jail by night to release the prisoners. Time and again we read of Abbots who refuse to join in a communal reproof of this or that delinquent, like Abbot Moses, that great gentle Negro, who walked into the severe assembly with a basket of sand, letting the sand run out through many holes. "My own sins are running out like this sand," he said, "and yet I come to judge the sins of another."

If such protests were made, there was obviously something to protest against. By the end of the fifth century Scete and Nitria had become rudimentary monastic cities, with laws and penalties. Three whips hung from a palm tree outside the church of Scete: one to punish delinquent monks, one to punish thieves and one for vagrants. But there were many monks like Abbot Moses who did not agree: and these were the saints. They represented the primitive "anarchic" desert ideal. Perhaps the most memorable of all were the two old brothers who had lived together for years without a quarrel, who decided to "get into an argument like the rest of men" but simply could not succeed.

Prayer was the very heart of the desert life, and consisted of psalmody (vocal prayer—recitation of the Psalms and other parts of the Scriptures which everyone had to know by heart) and contemplation. What we would call today contemplative prayer is referred to as *quies* or "rest." This illuminating term has persisted in Greek monastic tradition as *hesychia,* "sweet repose." *Quies* is a silent absorption aided by the soft repetition of a lone phrase of the Scriptures—the most popular being the prayer of the Publican: "Lord Jesus Christ, Son of God, have mercy on me a sinner!" In a shortened form this prayer became "Lord have mercy" *(Kyrie eleison)*—repeated interiorly hundreds of times a day until it became as spontaneous and instinctive as breathing.

When Arsenius is told to fly from the Cenobium, be silent and rest *(fuge, tace, quiesce)* it is a call to "contemplative prayer." *Quies* is a simpler and less pretentious term, and much less misleading. It suits the simplicity of the Desert Fathers much better than "contemplation" and affords less occasion for spiritual narcissism or megalomania. There was small danger of quietism in the desert. The monks were kept busy, and if *quies* was a fulfilment of all they sought, *corporalis quies* ("bodily rest") was one of their greatest enemies. I have translated *corporalis quies* as "an easy life," so as not to give the impression that agitated action was tolerated in the desert. It was not. The monk was supposed to remain tranquil and stay as much as possible in one place. Some Fathers even frowned on those who sought employment outside their cells and worked for the farmers of the Nile valley during the harvest season.

Finally, in these pages we meet several great and simple personalities. Though the *Verba* are sometimes ascribed only to an unidentified *senex* (elder) they are more often attributed by name to the saint who uttered them. We meet Abbot Anthony, who is no other than St. Anthony the Great. This is the Father of all hermits, whose biography, by St. Athanasius, set the whole Roman world afire with monastic vocations. Anthony was indeed the Father of all the Desert Fathers. But contact with his original thought reminds us that he is not the Anthony of Flaubert—nor do we find here anyone like the Paphnutius of Anatole France. Anthony, it is true, attained *apatheia* after long and somewhat spectacular contests with demons. But in the end he concluded that not even the devil was purely evil, since God could not create evil, and all His works are good. It may come as a surprise to learn that St. Anthony, of all people, thought the devil had some good in him. This was not mere sentimentalism. It showed that in Anthony there was not much room left for paranoia. We can profitably reflect that modern mass-man is the one who has returned so wholeheartedly to fanatical projections of all one's own evil upon "the enemy" (whoever that may be). The solitaries of the desert were much wiser.

Then in these *Verba* we meet others like St. Arsenius, the dour and silent stranger who came to the desert from the far-off court of the Emperors of Constantinople and would not let anybody see his face. We meet the gentle Poemen, the impetuous John the Dwarf, who wanted to "become an angel." Not the least attractive is Abbot Pastor, who appears perhaps most frequently of all. His sayings are distinguished by their practical humility, their understanding of human frailty and their solid common sense. Pastor, we know, was himself very human, and it is said of him that when his own blood brother seemed to grow cold to him and preferred the conversation of another hermit, he became so jealous that he had to go to one of the elders and get his sights adjusted.

These monks insisted on remaining human and "ordinary." This may seem to be a paradox, but it is very important. If we reflect a moment, we will see that to fly into the desert in order to be extraordinary is only to carry the world with you as an implicit standard of comparison. The result would be nothing but self-contemplation, and self-comparison with the negative standard of the world one had abandoned. Some of the monks of the desert did this, as a matter of fact: and the only fruit of their trouble was that they went out of their heads. The simple men who lived their lives out to a good old age among the rocks and sands only did so because they had come into the desert to be themselves, their *ordinary* selves, and to forget a world that divided them from themselves. There can be no other valid reason for seeking solitude or for leaving the world. And thus to leave the world, is, in fact, to help save it in saving oneself. This is the final point, and it is an important one. The Coptic hermits who left the world as though escaping from a wreck, did not merely intend to save themselves. They knew that they were helpless to do any good for others as long as they floundered about in the wreckage. But once they got a foothold on solid ground, things were different. Then they had not only the power but even the obligation to pull the whole world to safety after them.

This is their paradoxical lesson for our time. It would perhaps be too much to say that the world needs another movement such as that which drew these men into the deserts of Egypt and Palestine. Ours is certainly a time for solitaries and for hermits. But merely to reproduce the simplicity, austerity and prayer of these primitive souls is not a complete or satisfactory answer. We must transcend them, and transcend all those who, since their time, have gone beyond the limits which they set. We must liberate ourselves, in our own way, from involvement in a world that is plunging to disaster. But our world is different from theirs. Our involvement in it is more complete. Our danger is far more desperate. Our time, perhaps, is shorter than we think.

We cannot do exactly what they did. But we must be as thorough and as ruthless in our determination to break all spiritual chains, and cast off the domination of alien compulsions, to find our true selves, to discover and develop our inalienable spiritual liberty and use it to build, on earth, the Kingdom of God. This is not the place in which to speculate what our great and mysterious vocation might involve. That is still unknown. Let it suffice for me to say that we need to learn from these men of the fourth century how to ignore prejudice, defy compulsion and strike out fearlessly into the unknown.

Some Sayings of the Desert Fathers

I

ABBOT PAMBO questioned Abbot Anthony saying: What ought I to do? And the elder replied: Have no confidence in your own virtuousness. Do not worry about a thing once it has been done. Control your tongue and your belly.

II

ABBOT JOSEPH of Thebes said: There are three kinds of men who find honour in the sight of God: First, those who, when they are ill and tempted, accept all these things with thanksgiving. The second, those who do all their works clean in the sight of God, in no way merely seeking to please men. The third, those who sit in subjection to the command of a spiritual father and renounce all their own desires.

III

A BROTHER ASKED one of the elders: What good thing shall I do, and have life thereby? The old man replied: God alone knows what is good. However, I have heard it said that someone inquired of Father Abbot Nisteros the great, the friend of Abbot Anthony, asking: What good work shall I do? and that he replied: Not all works are alike. For Scripture says that Abraham was hospitable and God was with him. Elias loved solitary prayer, and God was with him. And David was humble, and God was with him. Therefore, whatever you see your soul to desire according to God, do that thing, and you shall keep your heart safe.

IV

ONE OF THE ELDERS SAID: Poverty, tribulation, and discretion: these are the three works of the hermit life. For it is written: If we but had with us these three men: Noe, Job and Daniel (see Ezechiel 14). Now Noe represents those who possess nothing. Job represents those who suffer tribulation. Daniel, those who discern good from evil. If these three actions are found in a man, then God dwells in him.

V

ABBOT PASTOR SAID: There are two things which a monk ought to hate above all, for by hating them he can become free in this world. And a brother asked: What are these things? The elder replied: An easy life and vain glory.

VI

THEY SAID OF ABBOT PAMBO that in the very hour when he departed this life he said to the holy men who stood by him: From the time I came to this place in the desert, and built me a cell, and dwelt here, I do not remember eating bread that was not earned by the work of my own hands, nor do I remember saying anything for which I was sorry even until this hour. And thus I go to the Lord as one who has not even made a beginning in the service of God.

VII

A BROTHER ASKED one of the elders: How does fear of the Lord get into a man? And the elder said: If a man have humility and poverty, and judge not another, that is how fear of the Lord gets into him.

VIII

ONCE SOME BRETHREN went out of the monastery to visit the hermits who lived in the desert. They came to one who received them with joy and seeing that they were tired, invited them to eat before the accustomed time and placed before them all the food he had available. But that night when they were all supposed to be sleeping the hermit heard the cenobites talking among themselves and saying: These hermits eat more than we do in the monastery. Now at dawn the guests set out to see another hermit, and as they were starting out their host said: Greet him from me, and give him this message: Be careful not to water the vegetables. When they reached the other hermitage they delivered this message. And the second hermit understood what was meant by the words. So he made the visitors sit down and weave baskets, and sitting with them he worked without interruption. And in the evening when the time came for lighting the lamp, he added a few extra psalms to the usual number, after which he said to them: We do not usually eat every day out here, but because you have come along it is fitting to have a little supper today, for a change. Then he gave them some dry bread and salt, then added: Here's a special treat for you. Upon which he mixed them a little sauce of vinegar, salt and oil, and gave it to them. After supper they got up again and started in on the psalms and kept on praying almost until dawn, at which the hermit said: Well, we can't finish all our usual prayers, for you are tired from your journey. You had better take a little rest. And so when the first hour of the day came, they all wanted to leave this hermit, but he would not let them go. He kept saying: Stay with me a while. I cannot let you go so soon, charity demands that I keep you for two or three days. But they, hearing this, waited until dark and then under cover of night they made off.

IX

AN ELDER SAID: Here is the monk's life-work, obedience, meditation, not judging others, not reviling, not complaining. For it is written: You who love the Lord, hate evil. So this is the monk's life— not to walk in agreement with an unjust man, nor to look with his eyes upon evil, nor to go about being curious, and neither to examine nor to listen to the business of others. Not to take anything with his hands, but rather to give to others. Not to be proud in his heart, nor to malign others in his thoughts. Not to fill his stomach, but in all things to behave with discretion. Behold, in all this you have the monk.

X

An elder said: Cut off from yourself rash confidence, and control your tongue and your belly, and abstain from wine. And if anyone speak to you about any matter do not argue with him. But if he speaks rightly, say: Yes. If he speaks wrongly say to him: You know what you are saying. But do not argue with him about the things he has said. Thus your mind will be at peace.

XI

ABBOT ANTHONY SAID: Just as fish die if they remain on dry land so monks, remaining away from their cells, or dwelling with men of the world, lose their determination to persevere in solitary prayer. Therefore, just as the fish should go back to the sea, so we must return to our cells, lest remaining outside we forget to watch over ourselves interiorly.

XII

ABBOT ARSENIUS, when he was still in the King's palace, prayed to the Lord saying: Lord, lead me to salvation. And a voice came to him saying: Arsenius, fly from men and you shall be saved. Again, embracing the monastic life, he prayed in the same words. And he heard a voice saying to him: Arsenius, fly, be silent, rest in prayer: these are the roots of non-sinning.

XIII

A CERTAIN BROTHER went to Abbot Moses in Scete, and asked him for a good word. And the elder said to him: Go, sit in your cell, and your cell will teach you everything.

XIV

AN ELDER SAW a certain one laughing and said to him: In the presence of the Lord of heaven and earth we must answer for our whole life; and you can laugh?

XV

IT WAS SAID of Abbot Agatho that for three years he carried a stone in his mouth until he learned to be silent.

XVI

ONE OF THE BRETHREN questioned Abbot Isidore, the elder of Scete, saying: Why is it that the demons are so grievously afraid of you? The elder replied: From the moment I became a monk I have striven to prevent anger rising to my lips.

XVII

ABBOT ANASTASIUS had a book written on very fine parchment which was worth eighteen pence, and had in it both the Old and New Testaments in full. Once a certain brother came to visit him, and seeing the book made off with it. So that day when Abbot Anastasius went to read his book, and found that it was gone, he realized that the brother had taken it. But he did not send after him to inquire about it for fear that the brother might add perjury to theft. Well, the brother went down into the nearby city in order to sell the book. And the price he asked was sixteen pence. The buyer said: Give me the book that I may find out whether it is worth that much. With that, the buyer took the book to the holy Anastasius and said: Father, take a look at this book, please, and tell me whether you think I ought to buy it for sixteen pence. Is it worth that much? Abbot Anastasius said: Yes, it is a fine book, it is worth that much. So the buyer went back to the brother and said: Here is your money. I showed the book to Abbot Anastasius and he said it is a fine book and is worth at least sixteen pence. But the brother asked: Was that all he said? Did he make any other remarks? No, said the buyer, he did not say another word. Well, said the brother, I have changed my mind and I don't want to sell this book after all. Then he hastened to Abbot Anastasius and begged him with tears to take back his book, but the Abbot would not accept it, saying: Go in peace, brother, I make you a present of it. But the brother said: If you do not take it back I shall never have any peace. After that the brother dwelt with Abbot Anastasius for the rest of his life.

XVIII

ABBOT MACARIUS SAID: If, wishing to correct another, you are moved to anger, you gratify your own passion. Do not lose yourself in order to save another.

XIX

Aввот Hyperichius said: It is better to eat meat and drink wine, than by detraction to devour the flesh of your brother.

XX

ONCE IN SCETE a bottle of wine from the new vintage was brought in, so that the brethren might have some, each in his goblet. One of the brethren came in and seeing that they had received wine, he ran and hid in the cellar. But the cellar caved in. When they had heard the noise, they ran and found the brother lying half dead, and they began to rebuke him, saying: It serves you right, because of your vanity. But the Abbot, giving him every care, said: Forgive my son, for he has done well. And as the Lord lives, this cellar shall not be built again in my time, so that the world may know that for the sake of a glass of wine a cellar collapsed in Scete.

XXI

A MONK RAN INTO A PARTY of handmaids of the Lord on a certain journey. Seeing them he left the road and gave them a wide berth. But the Abbess said to him: If you were a perfect monk, you would not even have looked close enough to see that we were women.

XXII

A CERTAIN BROTHER, renouncing the world, and giving the things he owned to the poor, kept a few things in his own possession. He came to Abbot Anthony. When the elder heard about all this, he said to him: If you want to be a monk, go to that village and buy meat, and place it on your naked body and so return here. And when the brother had done as he was told, dogs and birds of prey tore at his body. When he returned to the elder, the latter asked if he had done as he was told. The brother showed him his lacerated body. Then Abbot Anthony said: Those who renounce the world and want to retain possession of money are assailed and torn apart by devils just as you are.

XXIII

Abbot Theodore of Pherme had three good books. And when he had come to Abbot Macarius he said to him: I have three books, and I profit by reading them. Also the brethren ask to borrow them, and they profit also. Now tell me, what ought I to do? And the elder replied, saying: Those things that you do are good, but better than all else is to possess nothing. When he had heard this, he went off and sold the above-mentioned books, and gave their price to the poor.

XXIV

ABBOT AMMONAS SAID that he had spent fourteen years in Scete praying to God day and night to be delivered from anger.

XXV

ABBOT PASTOR SAID: The virtue of a monk is made manifest by temptations.

XXVI

AN ELDER SAID: The reason why we do not get anywhere is that we do not know our limits, and we are not patient in carrying on the work we have begun. But without any labour at all we want to gain possession of virtue.

XXVII

An elder said: Just as a tree cannot bear fruit if it is often transplanted, so neither can a monk bear fruit if he frequently changes his abode.

XXVIII

An elder said: The monk's cell is that furnace of Babylon in which the three children found the Son of God; but it is also the pillar of cloud, out of which God spoke to Moses.

XXIX

A CERTAIN BROTHER CAME, once, to Abbot Theodore of Pherme, and spent three days begging him to let him hear a word. The Abbot however did not answer him, and he went off sad. So a disciple said to Abbot Theodore: Father, why did you not speak to him? Now he has gone off sad! The elder replied: Believe me, I spoke no word to him because he is a trader in words, and seeks to glory in the words of another.

XXX

ANOTHER BROTHER ASKED the same elder, Abbot Theodore, and began to question him and to inquire about things which he had never yet put into practice himself. The elder said to him: As yet you have not found a ship, and you have not put your baggage aboard, and you have not started to cross the sea: can you talk as if you had already arrived in that city to which you planned to go? When you have put into practice the thing you are talking about, then speak from knowledge of the thing itself!

XXXI

Once a certain provincial judge heard of Abbot Moses and went off to Scete to see him. Someone told the elder that the visitor was coming and he rose up to fly into the marshes. But on the way he ran into the judge with his companions. The judge asked him, saying: Tell us, elder, where is the cell of Abbot Moses? The elder replied: What do you want with him? The man is a fool and a heretic! The judge went on and came to the church of Scete and said to the clerics: I heard about this Abbot Moses and came out here to meet him. And an old man heading for Eypgt ran into us, and we asked him where was the cell of Abbot Moses, and he said to us: What do you want with him? The man is a fool and a heretic! But the clerics, hearing this, were saddened and said: What kind of old man was this, who said such things to you about the holy man? They said: He was a very old elder with a long black robe. Then the clerics said: Why, that was Abbot Moses himself. And because he did not want to be seen by you, therefore he said those things about himself. Greatly edified, the judge returned home.

XXXII

Abbot Poeman said: Unless Nabuzardan the prince of the cooks had come to Jerusalem the temple of the Lord would not have been burnt with fire (IV Kings 25). So too, unless the desire of gluttony had come into the soul, the mind of man would not have been enkindled by the temptations of the devil.

XXXIII

A CERTAIN BROTHER came to Abbot Silvanus at Mount Sinai, and seeing the hermits at work he exclaimed: Why do you work for the bread that perisheth? Mary has chosen the best part, namely to sit at the feet of the Lord without working. Then the Abbot said to his disciple Zachary: Give the brother a book and let him read, and put him in an empty cell. At the ninth hour the brother who was reading began to look out to see if the Abbot was not going to call him to dinner, and sometime after the ninth hour he went himself to the Abbot and said: Did the brethren not eat today, Father? Oh yes, certainly, said the Abbot, they just had dinner. Well, said the brother, why did you not call me? You are a spiritual man, said the elder, you don't need this food that perisheth. We have to work, but you have chosen the best part. You read all day, and can get along without food. Hearing this the brother said: Forgive me, Father. And the elder said: Martha is necessary to Mary, for it was because Martha worked that Mary was able to be praised.

XXXIV

ONE OF THE MONKS, called Serapion, sold his book of the Gospels and gave the money to those who were hungry, saying: I have sold the book which told me to sell all that I had and give to the poor.

XXXV

ONE OF THE BRETHREN had been insulted by another and he wanted to take revenge. He came to Abbot Sisois and told him what had taken place, saying: I am going to get even, Father. But the elder besought him to leave the affair in the hands of God. No, said the brother, I will not give up until I have made that fellow pay for what he said. Then the elder stood up and began to pray in these terms: O God, Thou art no longer necessary to us, and we no longer need Thee to take care of us since, as this brother says, we both can and will avenge ourselves. At this the brother promised to give up his idea of revenge.

XXXVI

ONE OF THE BROTHERS asked Abbot Sisois: Supposing some robbers or savages attack me and try to kill me: if I can overcome them should I kill them myself? The elder replied: Not at all. But commit yourself entirely to God. Any evil that comes to you, confess that it has happened to you because of your sins, for you must learn to attribute everything to the dispensation of God's wisdom.

XXXVII

THERE WAS ONCE A GREAT HERMIT in the mountains and he was attacked by robbers. But his cries aroused the other hermits in the neighbourhood, and they ran together and captured the robbers. These they sent under guard to the town and the judge put them in jail. But then the brothers were very ashamed and sad because, on their account, the robbers had been turned over to the judge. They went to Abbot Poemen and told him all about it. And the elder wrote to the hermit saying: Remember who carried out the first betrayal, and you will learn the reason for the second. Unless you had first been betrayed by your own inward thoughts, you would never have ended by turning those men over to the judge. The hermit, touched by these words, got up at once and went into the city and broke open the jail, letting out the robbers and freeing them from torture.

XXXVIII

O NCE THERE WAS A DISCIPLE of a Greek philosopher who was commanded by his Master for three years to give money to everyone who insulted him. When this period of trial was over, the Master said to him: Now you can go to Athens and learn wisdom. When the disciple was entering Athens he met a certain wise man who sat at the gate insulting everybody who came and went. He also insulted the disciple who immediately burst out laughing. Why do you laugh when I insult you? said the wise man. Because, said the disciple, for three years I have been paying for this kind of thing and now you give it to me for nothing. Enter the city, said the wise man, it is all yours. Abbot John used to tell the above story, saying: This is the door of God by which our fathers rejoicing in many tribulations enter into the City of Heaven.

XXXIX

ONCE IN THE VALLEY OF THE CELLS, a feast being celebrated, the brethren were eating together in the place of assembly. And there was a certain brother present, who said to the one waiting on table: I do not eay any cooked food, just a little salt.[1] And the one waiting on table called another brother in the presence of the whole assembly, saying: That brother does not eat cooked food. Just bring him some salt. One of the elders got up and said to the brother who wanted salt: It would have been better had you eaten meat alone in your cell today, than to let this thing be heard in the presence of so many brethren.

XL

ONE OF THE BRETHREN HAD SINNED, and the priest told him to leave the community. So then Abbot Bessarion got up and walked out with him, saying: I too am a sinner!

XLI

A BROTHER IN SCETE happened to commit a fault, and the elders assembled, and sent for Abbot Moses to join them. He, however, did not want to come. The priest sent him a message, saying: Come, the community of the brethren is waiting for you. So he arose and started off. And taking with him a very old basket full of holes, he filled it with sand, and carried it behind him. The elders came out to meet him, and said: What is this, Father? The elder replied: My sins are running out behind me, and I do not see them, and today I come to judge the sins of another! They, hearing this, said nothing to the brother but pardoned him.

XLII

A CERTAIN BROTHER INQUIRED of Abbot Pastor, saying: What shall I do? I lose my nerve when I am sitting alone at prayer in my cell. The elder said to him: Despise no one, condemn no one, rebuke no one, God will give you peace and your meditation will be undisturbed.

XLIII

AN ELDER SAID: Do not judge a fornicator if you are chaste, for if you do, you too are violating the law as much as he is. For He who said thou shalt not fornicate also said thou shalt not judge.

XLIV

ONE OF THE FATHERS told a story of a certain elder who was in his cell busily at work and wearing a hair shirt when Abbot Ammonas came to him. When Abbot Ammonas saw him wearing a hair shirt he said: That thing won't do you a bit of good. The elder said: Three thoughts are troubling me. The first impels me to withdraw somewhere into the wilderness. The second, to seek a foreign land where no one knows me. The third, to wall myself into this cell and see no one and eat only every second day. Abbot Ammonas said to him: None of these three will do you a bit of good. But rather sit in your cell, and eat a little every day, and have always in your heart the words which are read in the Gospel and were said by the Publican,[2] and thus you can be saved.

XLV

IT WAS TOLD OF ABBOT JOHN the Dwarf that once he had said to his elder brother: I want to live in the same security as the angels have, doing no work, but serving God without intermission. And casting off everything he had on, he started out into the desert. When a week had gone by he returned to his brother. And while he was knocking on the door, his brother called out before opening, and asked: Who are you? He replied: I am John. Then his brother answered and said: John has become an angel and is no longer among men. But John kept on knocking and said: It is I. Still the brother did not open, but kept him waiting. Finally, opening the door, he said: If you are a man, you are going to have to start working again in order to live. But if you are an angel, why do you want to come into a cell? So John did penance and said: Forgive me, brother, for I have sinned.

XLVI

ABBOT PASTOR SAID: If you have a chest full of clothing, and leave it for a long time, the clothing will rot inside it. It is the same with the thoughts in our heart. If we do not carry them out by physical action, after a long while they will spoil and turn bad.

XLVII

THE SAME FATHER SAID: If there are three monks living together, of whom one remains silent in prayer at all times, and another is ailing and gives thanks for it, and the third waits on them both with sincere good will, these three are equal, as if they were performing the same work.

XLVIII

He said, again: Malice will never drive out malice. But if someone does evil to you, you should do good to him, so that by your good work you may destroy his malice.

XLIX

AND HE ALSO SAID: He who is quarrelsome is no monk: he who returns evil for evil is no monk: he who gets angry is no monk.

L

A brother came to Abbot Pastor and said: Many distracting thoughts come into my mind, and I am in danger because of them. Then the elder thrust him out into the open air and said: Open up the garments about your chest and catch the wind in them. But he replied: This I cannot do. So the elder said to him: If you cannot catch the wind, neither can you prevent distracting thoughts from coming into your head. Your job is to say No to them.

LI

ABBOT AMMONAS SAID: One man carries an axe all his life and never cuts down a tree. Another, who knows how to cut, gives a few swings and the tree is down. This axe, he said, is discretion.

LII

A BROTHER INQUIRED of Abbot Pastor saying: My soul suffers harm from living with the Spiritual Father that I have. What, then, do you command me to do? Shall I go on staying with him? Now Abbot Pastor knew that the brother's soul would be harmed by this other Abbot, and he was surprised that he even asked whether he ought to go on staying with him. And he said to him: If you like, stay with him. The brother went off and remained with that Father. But he came back again, saying to Abbot Pastor: It is a great burden on my soul! And still Abbot Pastor did not tell him to leave the man. Finally the brother came back a third time and said: Believe me, I am through with him! Then the elder said: See! now you are saved, go, and have no more to do with him. And Abbot Pastor told the same brother: When a man sees that his soul is suffering harm, he has no need to ask advice about it. When it is a matter of secret thoughts, one asks advice, that the elders may test them. But when there are manifest sins there is no need to inquire—you just break off at once.

LIII

ABBOT PALLADIUS SAID: The soul that wishes to live according to the will of Christ should either learn faithfully what it does not yet know, or teach openly what it does know. But if, when it can, it desires to do neither of these things, it is afflicted with madness. For the first step away from God is a distaste for learning, and lack of appetite for those things for which the soul hungers when it seeks God.

LIV

ONE OF THE ELDERS SAID: If a man settles in a certain place and does not bring forth the fruit of that place, the place itself casts him out, as one who has not borne its fruit.

LV

An elder was asked: What does it mean, this word we read in the Bible, that the way is strait and narrow? And the elder replied: This is the strait and narrow way: that a man should do violence to his judgments and cut off, for the love of God, the desires of his own will. This is what was written of the Apostles: Behold we have left all things and have followed Thee.

LVI

ONE OF THE ELDERS SAID: It is not because evil thoughts come to us that we are condemned, but only because we make use of the evil thoughts. It can happen that from these thoughts we suffer shipwreck, but it can also happen that because of them we may be crowned.

LVII

ANOTHER ELDER SAID: It happens that one man eats more and yet remains hungry, and another man eats less, and is satisfied. The greater reward belongs to the one who ate more and is still hungry than to him who ate less and is satisfied.

LVIII

THERE WAS A CERTAIN BROTHER who was praised by all the others in the presence of Abbot Anthony, but when the elder tested him he found that he could not bear to be insulted. Then Abbot Anthony said: You, brother, are like a house with a big strong gate, that is freely entered by robbers through all the windows.

LIX

A CERTAIN BROTHER CAME to Abbot Poemen and said: What ought I to do, Father? I am in great sadness. The elder said to him: Never despise anybody, never condemn anybody, never speak evil of anyone, and the Lord will give you peace.

LX

ONE OF THE BRETHREN ASKED an elder, saying: Father, do the holy men always know when the power of God is in them? And the elder replied: No, they do not always know it. For once a very great hermit had a disciple who did something wrong and the hermit said to him: Go and drop dead! Instantly the disciple fell down dead and the hermit, overcome with terror, prayed to the Lord, saying: Lord Jesus Christ, I beg Thee to bring my disciple back to life and from now on I will be careful what I say. Then right away the disciple was restored to life.

LXI

ONE OF THE ELDERS used to say: In the beginning when we got together we used to talk about something that was good for our souls, and we went up and up, and ascended even to heaven. But now we get together and spend our time in criticizing everything, and we drag one another down into the abyss.

LXII

YET ANOTHER ELDER SAID: If you see a young
monk by his own will climbing up into heaven,
take him by the foot and throw him to the ground,
because what he is doing is not good for him.

LXIII

ABBOT BESSARION, dying, said: The monk should be all eye, like the cherubim and seraphim.

LXIV

ABBOT PASTOR SAID: Get away from any man who always argues every time he talks.

LXV

A CERTAIN ELDER SAID: Apply yourself to silence, have no vain thoughts, and be intent in your meditation, whether you sit at prayer, or whether you rise up to work in the fear of God. If you do these things, you will not have to fear the attacks of the evil ones.

LXVI

ANOTHER OF THE ELDERS SAID: When the eyes of an ox or mule are covered, then he goes round and round turning the mill wheel: but if his eyes are uncovered he will not go around in the circle of the mill wheel. So too the devil if he manages to cover the eyes of a man, he can humiliate him in every sin. But if that man's eyes are not closed, he can easily escape from the devil.

LXVII

CERTAIN BRETHREN CAME from the Thebaid to buy linen, and they said to one another: This opportunity will enable us to see the Blessed Arsenius. But when they came to his cave, his disciple Daniel went in and told him of their wish. Arsenius replied: Go, my son, receive them and do them honour. But permit me to look upon heaven, and let them go their way. My face they shall not see.

LXVIII

THE HOLY FATHERS came together and spoke of what would happen in the last generation, and one of them especially, called Squirion, said: We now fulfil the commandments of God. Then the Fathers asked him: What about those who will come after us? He replied: Perhaps half of them will keep the commandments of God and will seek the eternal God. And the Fathers asked: Those who come after these, what shall they do? He replied and said: The men of that generation will not have the works of God's commandments and will forget His precepts. At that time wickedness will overflow and the charity of many will grow cold. And there shall come upon them a terrible testing. Those who shall be found worthy in this testing will be better than we are and better than our fathers. They shall be happier and more perfectly proven in virtue.

LXIX

ABBOT ARSENIUS lived in a cell thirty-two miles away from his nearest neighbour, and he seldom went out of it. The things he needed were brought there by disciples. But when the desert of Scete where he lived became peopled with hermits, he went away from there weeping and saying: Worldly men have ruined Rome and monks have ruined Scete.

LXX

Abraham, the disciple of Abbot Sisois, said to him: Father, you are an old man. Let's go back to the world. Abbot Sisois replied: Very well, we'll go where there are no women. His disciple said: What is the place in which there are no women, except the desert alone? The elder replied to him: Therefore take me into the desert.

LXXI

THE STORY IS TOLD that one of the elders lay dying in Scete, and the brethren surrounded his bed, dressed him in the shroud, and began to weep. But he opened his eyes and laughed. He laughed another time, and then a third time. When the brethren saw this, they asked him, saying: Tell us, Father, why you are laughing while we weep? He said to them: I laughed the first time because you fear death. I laughed the second time because you are not ready for death. And the third time I laughed because from labours I go to my rest. As soon as he had said this, he closed his eyes in death.

LXXII

Abbot Lot came to Abbot Joseph and said: Father, according as I am able, I keep my little rule, and my little fast, my prayer, meditation and contemplative silence; and according as I am able I strive to cleanse my heart of thoughts: now what more should I do? The elder rose up in reply and stretched out his hands to heaven, and his fingers became like ten lamps of fire. He said: Why not be totally changed into fire?

LXXIII

THEY USED TO SAY of Abbot Sisois that unless he quickly lowered his hands and ceased from praying, his mind would be carried away into heaven. And whenever he happened to pray with another brother, he made haste to lower his hands lest his mind be carried away and he remain in another world.

LXXIV

ONE OF THE FATHERS SAID: Just as it is impossible for a man to see his face in troubled water, so too the soul, unless it be cleansed of alien thoughts, cannot pray to God in contemplation.

LXXV

A BROTHER CAME and stayed with a certain solitary and when he was leaving he said: Forgive me, Father, for I have broken in upon your Rule. But the hermit replied, saying: My Rule is to receive you with hospitality and to let you go in peace.

LXXVI

A BROTHER SAID TO ABBOT PASTOR: If I give one of my brothers a little bread or something of the sort, the demons spoil everything and it seems to me that I have acted only to please men. The elder said to him: Even if your good work was done to please, we must still give to our brothers what they need. And he told him this story. Two farmers lived in a village. One of them sowed his field and reaped only a small and wretched crop. The other neglected to sow anything at all, and so he reaped nothing. Which of the two will survive, if there is a famine? The brother replied: The first one, even though his crop is small and wretched. The elder said to him: Let us also sow, even though our sowing is small and wretched, lest we die in the time of hunger.

LXXVII

ABBOT HYPERICHIUS SAID: The office of a monk is to obey, and if he fulfils it, what he asks in prayer will be granted, and he will stand with confidence before the Crucified Christ: for thus the Lord Himself came to His Cross, being made obedient unto death.

LXXVIII

Some elders once came to Abbot Anthony, and there was with them also Abbot Joseph. Wishing to test them, Abbot Anthony brought the conversation around to the Holy Scriptures. And he began from the youngest to ask them the meaning of this or that text. Each one replied as best he could, but Abbot Anthony said to them: You have not got it yet. After them all he asked Abbot Joseph: What about you? What do you say this text means? Abbot Joseph replied: I know not! Then Abbot Anthony said: Truly Abbot Joseph alone has found the way, for he replies that he knows not.

LXXIX

John of Thebes said: The monk must be before all else humble. This is the first commandment of the Lord, who said: Blessed are the poor of spirit, for theirs is the Kingdom of Heaven.

LXXX

Once Abbot Macarius was on his way home to his cell from the marshes, carrying reeds, and he met the devil with a reaper's sickle in his path. The devil tried to get him with the sickle, and couldn't. And he said: I suffer great violence from you, Macarius, because I cannot overcome you. For see, I do all the things that you do. You fast, and I eat nothing at all. You watch, and I never sleep. But there is one thing alone in which you overcome me. Abbot Macarius said to him: What is that? Your humility, the devil replied, for because of it I cannot overcome you.

LXXXI

ABBOT PASTOR was asked by a certain brother:
How should I conduct myself in the place where
I live? The elder replied: Be as cautious as a
stranger; wherever you may be, do not desire your
word to have power before you, and you will have
rest.

LXXXII

Abbot Pastor said: A man must breathe humility and the fear of God just as ceaselessly as he inhales and exhales the air.

LXXXIII

ABBOT ALONIUS SAID: Humility is the land where God wants us to go and offer sacrifice.

LXXXIV

ONE OF THE ELDERS was asked what was humility, and he said: If you forgive a brother who has injured you before he himself asks pardon.

LXXXV

A BROTHER ASKED one of the elders: What is humility? The elder answered him: To do good to those who do evil to you. The brother asked: Supposing a man cannot go that far, what should he do? The elder replied: Let him get away from them and keep his mouth shut.

LXXXVI

To one of the brethren appeared a devil, transformed into an angel of light, who said to him: I am the Angel Gabriel, and I have been sent to thee. But the brother said: Think again—you must have been sent to somebody else. I haven't done anything to deserve an angel. Immediately the devil ceased to appear.

LXXXVII

IT WAS SAID OF ONE of the elders that he perse-
vered in a fast of seventy weeks, eating only once
a week. This elder asked God to reveal to him
the meaning of a certain Scripture text, and God
would not reveal it to him. So he said to himself:
Look at all the work I have done without getting
anywhere! I will go to one of the brothers and ask
him. When he had gone out and closed the door
and was starting on his way an angel of the Lord
was sent to him, saying: The seventy weeks you
fasted did not bring you any closer to God, but
now that you have humbled yourself and set out to
ask your brother, I am sent to reveal the meaning
of that text. And opening to him the meaning
which he sought, he went away.

LXXXVIII

Abbot Pastor said: Any trial whatever that comes to you can be conquered by silence.

LXXXIX

ABBESS SYNCLETICA of holy memory said: There is labour and great struggle for the impious who are converted to God, but after that comes inexpressible joy. A man who wants to light a fire first is plagued by smoke, and the smoke drives him to tears, yet finally he gets the fire that he wants. So also it is written: Our God is a consuming fire. Hence we ought to light the divine fire in ourselves with labour and with tears.

XC

ONCE THERE WAS AN ELDER in the lower parts of
Egypt, and he was a very famous hermit, living all
alone in a desert place. Satan brought it about that
a woman of easy virtue said to some young men:
What will you give me, and I will go out and knock
down that hermit of yours. So they agreed on a certain sum they would give her. And going out one
evening she came to his cell pretending to have
lost her way. She knocked at his door and he came
out. Seeing her he was disturbed and said: How
did you get out here? She pretended to weep, and
said: I have lost my way. So, being moved to pity,
he let her in to the front room of his cell, and for
his part he went on to the inner room and locked
the door. But the unfortunate woman cried out:
Father, the wild animals will eat me out here.
Once again the elder was disturbed and thought
of the Judgment of God, and said: How did this
dreadful thing ever happen to me? But, opening
his door, he let her in. And the devil began to shoot
flaming arrows into his heart. But he said within

himself: The ways of the enemy are darkness, and the Son of God is light. So he lit a lantern. But the temptation continued and he said to himself: Well, let's see whether you will be able to bear the flames of hell. And he put a finger into the flame. But though the flame burned him he did not feel it, so strong was the fire of lust in him. And he went on like that until morning, burning all his fingers. The unfortunate woman, watching what he was doing, was so struck with terror that she almost turned into stone. In the morning the two young men came to the hermit and said: Did a woman come here last night? Yes, said the hermit, she is over there asleep. But they said: Father, she is dead! Then he, throwing back the cloak he had on, showed them his hands and said: Look what she did to me, that child of hell! She has cost me all my fingers. And having told them all that had taken place he ended with: It is written thou shalt not render evil for evil. So he said a prayer and she revived. She was converted, and lived chastely for the rest of her life.

XCI

ABBOT PASTOR SAID that Abbot John the Dwarf had prayed to the Lord and the Lord had taken away all his passions, so that he became impassible. And in this condition he went to one of the elders and said: You see before you a man who is completely at rest and has no more temptations. The elder said: Go and pray to the Lord to command some struggle to be stirred up in you, for the soul is matured only in battles. And when the temptations started up again he did not pray that the struggle be taken away from him, but only said: Lord, give me strength to get through the fight.

XCII

ONCE ABBOT MACARIUS was travelling down from Scete to a place called Terenuthin, and he went to spend the night in a pyramid where the bodies of the pagans had been laid to rest years before. And he dragged out one of the mummies and put it under his head for a pillow. The devils, seeing his boldness, flew into a rage and decided to scare him. And they began to call out from the other bodies, as if calling to a woman: Lady, come with us to the baths. And another demon, as if he were the ghost of a woman, cried out from the body the elder was using as a pillow: This stranger is holding me down and I can't come. But the elder, far from being frightened, began to pummel the corpse, saying: Get up and go swimming if you are able. Hearing this the demons cried: You win! And they fled in confusion.

XCIII

I<small>T WAS TOLD OF</small> A<small>BBOT</small> M<small>ILIDO</small> that when he
lived in Persia with two disciples, the sons of the
Emperor went out on a great hunt, spreading nets
for forty miles around, determined to kill everything they caught in them. And the elder was found
in the nets with his two disciples. And when they
saw him all hairy (he was an awful sight!), they
were amazed and asked him whether he were a
man or some kind of spirit. He replied: I am a man
and a sinner and I came out here to weep for my
sins and to adore the Son of the Living God. To
which they replied: There is no god but sun and
water and fire. Adore these, and sacrifice to them.
Oh no I will not, he said, these are creatures and
you are mistaken. You should acknowledge the true
God who made these things and everything else
besides. A condemned and crucified criminal is
what you call a God! they said, mocking him. He
who was crucified destroyed death, said the elder,
and Him I call the true God. So they took him and
set him up like a target and shot arrows at him from

different sides, and while they were doing this the elder said to them: Tomorrow in this very hour your mother will be childless. They laughed at him, and started out the next day to continue hunting. And it happened that a stag got through the nets and they went after him on horseback, and coming towards the stag from opposite sides they let fly their arrows and struck one another in the heart and so died, according to the words of the elder.

XCIV

ONCE SOME ROBBERS came into the monastery and said to one of the elders: We have come to take away everything that is in your cell. And he said: My sons, take all you want. So they took everything they could find in the cell and started off. But they left behind a little bag that was hidden in the cell. The elder picked it up and followed after them, crying out: My sons, take this, you forgot it in the cell! Amazed at the patience of the elder, they brought everything back into his cell and did penance, saying: This one really is a man of God!

XCV

THERE WAS AN ELDER who had a well-tried novice living with him, and once, when he was annoyed, he drove the novice out of the cell. But the novice sat down outside and waited for the elder. The elder, opening the door, found him there, and did penance before him, saying: You are my Father, because your patience and humility have overcome the weakness of my soul. Come back in; you can be the elder and the Father, I will be the youth and the novice: for by your good work you have surpassed my old age.

XCVI

A BROTHER ASKED one of the elders, saying: There are two brothers, of whom one remains praying in his cell, fasting six days at a time and doing a great deal of penance. The other one takes care of the sick. Which one's work is more pleasing to God? The elder replied: If that brother who fasts six days at a time were to hang himself up by the nose, he could not equal the one who takes care of the sick.

XCVII

ABBOT AGATHO frequently admonished his disciple, saying: Never acquire for yourself anything that you might hesitate to give to your brother if he asked you for it, for thus you would be found a transgressor of God's command. If anyone asks, give to him, and if anyone wants to borrow from you, do not turn away from him.

XCVIII

A CERTAIN BROTHER ASKED of an elder, saying: If a brother owes me a little money, do you think I should ask him to pay me back? The elder said to him: Ask him for it once only, and with humility. The brother said: Suppose I ask him once and he doesn't give me anything, what should I do? Then the elder said: Don't ask him any more. The brother said again: But what can I do, I cannot get rid of my anxieties about it, unless I go and ask him? The elder said to him: Forget your anxieties. The important thing is not to sadden your brother, for you are a monk.

XCIX

When people came to buy from Abbot Agatho the things which he had made with the work of his hands, he sold to them in peace. His price for a sieve was a hundred pence, and for a basket two hundred and fifty. When they came to buy he told them the price, and took whatever they gave him, in silence, not even counting the coins. For he said: What is the use of me arguing with them, and leading them perhaps into sin by perjuring themselves and then, perhaps, if I have some extra money, giving it to the brethren? God does not want alms of this kind from me and it does not please Him if, in order to make my offering, I lead someone into sin. Then one of the brethren said to him: And how are you ever going to get a supply of bread for your cell? To which he answered: What need have I, in my cell, of the bread of men?

C

THERE WAS A CERTAIN ELDER who, if anyone maligned him, would go in person to offer him presents, if he lived nearby. And if he lived at a distance he would send presents by the hand of another.

CI

Aʙʙᴏᴛ Aɴᴛʜᴏɴʏ ᴛᴀᴜɢʜᴛ Abbot Ammonas, saying: You must advance yet further in the fear of
God. And taking him out of the cell he showed
him a stone, saying: Go and insult that stone, and
beat it without ceasing. When this had been done,
St. Anthony asked him if the stone had answered
back. No, said Ammonas. Then Abbot Anthony
said: You too must reach **the point** where you no
longer take offence at **anything**.

CII

ABBOT PASTOR SAID: Just as bees are driven out by smoke, and their honey is taken away from them, so a life of ease drives out the fear of the Lord from man's soul and takes away all his good works.

CIII

A CERTAIN PHILOSOPHER asked St. Anthony: Father, how can you be so happy when you are deprived of the consolation of books? Anthony replied: My book, O philosopher, is the nature of created things, and any time I want to read the words of God, the book is before me.

CIV

ONCE A CERTAIN PROVINCIAL JUDGE came to see Abbot Simon, and the elder took the belt he had on and went up to the top of a date palm as though he were a workman picking dates. But they, approaching, asked him: Where is the hermit who lives in this part of the desert? To which he replied: There is no hermit around here. At this they all departed. On another occasion a different judge came to see him, and his companions, running on ahead of the judge, said: Father, get ready. A judge who has heard about you is on his way out here to ask your blessing. The elder said: You can be sure I will get ready. And covering himself with all his garments he took some bread and cheese in his hands and sat down in the entry to his cell and began to eat. The judge and his retainers arrived and saw him eating and hailed him with contempt. Is this the hermit monk we heard so much about? they asked. They swung around immediately and headed back where they had come from.

CV

ABBOT JOSEPH ASKED ABBOT PASTOR: Tell me
how I can become a monk. The elder replied: If
you want to have rest here in this life and also in
the next, in every conflict with another say: Who
am I? And judge no one.

CVI

ONCE ABBOT ANTHONY was conversing with some brethren, and a hunter who was after game in the wilderness came upon them. He saw Abbot Anthony and the brothers enjoying themselves, and disapproved. Abbot Anthony said: Put an arrow in your bow and shoot it. This he did. Now shoot another, said the elder. And another, and another. The hunter said: If I bend my bow all the time it will break. Abbot Anthony replied: So it is also in the work of God. If we push ourselves beyond measure, the brethren will soon collapse. It is right, therefore, from time to time, to relax their efforts.

CVII

ONE OF THE HOLY FATHERS said to the monks who asked him about the reason for renunciation: My sons, it is right that we should hate all rest in this present life, and hate also pleasures of the body and the joys of the belly. Let us not seek honour from men: then Our Lord Jesus Christ will give us heavenly honours, rest in eternal life, and glorious joy with His angels.

CVIII

ABBOT ZENO TOLD US that once when he was on his way to Palestine he sat down under a tree, weary with journeying. Now he was right next to a field full of cucumbers. In his heart he thought to get up and help himself to the cucumbers, to repair his strength. For, he said, it would be no great thing to take a few of them. But replying to himself in his thoughts, he said: When thieves are condemned by the judges they are given over to torture. So I ought to test myself and see if I can stand the torments which are suffered by robbers. And rising up at that very hour he stood in the hot sun for five days and roasted his body. Then he said in his thoughts: I could not stand the torments, hence I ought not to steal, but to work with my hands according to the custom, and live on the fruit of my labour, as the Holy Scripture says: Because thou shalt eat of the work of thy hands, blessed shalt thou be, and it shall be well with thee. This, certainly, is what we sing every day in the sight of the Lord!

CIX

THE ELDERS AND ALL THE MONKS dwelling in the desert of Scete came together in council and agreed that Father Isaac should be ordained priest to serve the Church in that solitary place, where at stated days and hours the monks living in the desert come together for worship. But Abbot Isaac, hearing the decision that had been taken, fled to Egypt and hid himself in a field among the bushes, deeming himself unworthy of the honour of the priesthood. A large number of the monks set out after him, to catch him. Now when they had stopped at evening in that same field to rest, weary with their journey (for it was now night), they turned loose the ass that carried their baggage, and let him eat grass. Now while the ass was feeding, he came to the place where Abbot Isaac was hiding. And at daybreak, the monks, in search of the ass, came to the place where the old man had hidden himself. Marvelling at the dispensation of God, they seized him and were about to tie him up and take him prisoner and lead him away. But the venerable elder did not allow them, saying: Now I can no longer oppose you since it is perhaps the will of God that I, though unworthy, should receive priestly orders.

CX

THERE WERE TWO BROTHER MONKS living together in a cell and their humility and patience was praised by many of the Fathers. A certain holy man, hearing of this, wanted to test them and see if they possessed true and perfect humility. So he came to visit them. They received him with joy, and all together they said their prayers and their psalms, as usual. Then the visitor went outside the cell and saw their little garden, where they grew their vegetables. Seizing his stick, he rushed in with all his might and began to destroy every plant in sight so that soon there was nothing left at all. Seeing him the two brothers said not one word. They did not even show sad or troubled faces. Coming back into the cell they finished their prayers for Vespers, and paid him honour, saying: Sir, if you like, we can get one cabbage that is left, and cook it and eat it, for now it is time to eat. Then the elder fell down before them, saying: I give thanks to my God, for I see the Holy Spirit rests in you.

CXI

ONE OF THE BROTHERS ASKED an elder saying: Would it be all right if I kept two pence in my possession, in case I should get sick? The elder, seeing his thoughts and that he wanted to keep them, said: Keep them. The brother, going back to his cell, began to wrestle with his own thoughts, saying: I wonder if the Father gave me his blessing or not? Rising up, he went back to the Father, inquiring of him and saying: In God's name, tell me the truth, because I am all upset over these two pence. The elder said to him: Since I saw your thoughts and your desire to keep them, I told you to keep them. But it is not good to keep more than we need for our body. Now these two pence are your hope. If they should be lost, would not God take care of you? Cast your care upon the Lord, then, for He will take care of us.

CXII

THERE WERE TWO ELDERS living together in a cell, and they had never had so much as one quarrel with one another. One therefore said to the other: Come on, let us have at least one quarrel, like other men. The other said: I don't know how to start a quarrel. The first said: I will take this brick and place it here between us. Then I will say: It is mine. After that you will say: It is mine. This is what leads to a dispute and a fight. So then they placed the brick between them, one said: It is mine, and the other replied to the first: I do believe that it is mine. The first one said again: It is not yours, it is mine. So the other answered: Well then, if it is yours, take it! Thus they did not manage after all to get into a quarrel.

CXIII

ABBOT MARK ONCE SAID to Abbot Arsenius: It is good, is it not, to have nothing in your cell that just gives you pleasure? For example, once I knew a brother who had a little wildflower that came up in his cell, and he pulled it out by the roots. Well, said Abbot Arsenius, that is all right. But each man should act according to his own spiritual way. And if one were not able to get along without the flower, he should plant it again.

CXIV

ONCE THEY ASKED ABBOT AGATHO: Which is greater? Bodily asceticism, or watchfulness over the interior man? The elder said: A man is like a tree. His bodily works are like the leaves of the tree, but interior self-custody is like the fruits. Since, then, it is written that every tree not bearing good fruit shall be cut down and cast into the fire, we must take all care to bear this fruit, which is custody of the mind. But we also need leaves to cover and adorn us: and that means good works done with the aid of the body. This Abbot Agatho was wise in understanding and tireless in his work and ready for everything. He applied himself energetically to manual labour, and was sparing in his food and clothing.

CXV

THE SAME ABBOT AGATHO would say: Even if an angry man were to revive the dead, he would not be pleasing to God because of his anger.

CXVI

THERE WAS A CERTAIN ELDER who had fasted valiantly for fifty years and he said: I have put out the flames of lust, and avarice and vainglory. Abbot Abraham heard about it, and came to him asking: Did you really say that? I did, he replied. Then Abbot Abraham said: So you go into your cell, and there is a woman lying on your mat. Can you think that she is not a woman? He said, No, but I fight my thoughts so that I don't touch that woman. Then, said Abbot Abraham, you have not killed fornication. The passion is alive, but it is bound. And now supposing you are on a journey and in the road among the stones and broken pottery you see some gold: can you think of it as if it were like the other stones? No, he replied, but I resist my thoughts so that I do not pick it up. Then Abbot Abraham said: You see, the passion is alive. But it is bound. Then Abbot Abraham said again: You hear about two brothers, of whom one likes you and speaks well of you and the other hates you and speaks evil of you. They come to you: and do you receive them both alike? No, he replied, but I am tormented inside, trying to be just as nice to the one who hates me as I am to the other. Abbot Abraham said: The passions live, then. But in the saints they are only, to some extent, bound.

CXVII

IN THE BEGINNING of his conversion Abbot Evagrius[3] came to a certain elder and said: Father, tell me some word by which I may be saved. The elder said: If you want to be saved, whenever you go to see anybody do not speak until he asks you something. Evagrius was deeply moved by this saying, and did penance in the sight of the elder and made satisfaction to him, saying: Believe me, I have read many books and have never found anywhere such learning. And he went away and progressed greatly.

CXVIII

ONCE SOME OF THE ELDERS came to Scete, and Abbot John the Dwarf was with them. And when they were dining, one of the priests, a very great old man, got up to give each one a little cup of water to drink, and no one would take it from him except John the Dwarf. The others were surprised, and afterwards they asked him: How is it that you, the least of all, have presumed to accept the services of this great old man? He replied: Well, when I get up to give people a drink of water, I am happy if they all take it; and for that reason on this occasion I took the drink, that he might be rewarded, and not feel sad because nobody accepted the cup from him. And at this all admired his discretion.

CXIX

ONCE TWO BROTHERS were sitting with Abbot Poemen and one praised the other brother saying: He is a good brother, he hates evil. The old man said: What do you mean, he hates evil? And the brother did not know what to reply. So he said: Tell me, Father, what it is to hate evil? The Father said: That man hates evil who hates his own sins, and looks upon every brother as a saint, and loves him as a saint.

CXX

ABBOT JOHN USED TO SAY: We have thrown down a light burden, which is the reprehending of our own selves, and we have chosen instead to bear a heavy burden, by justifying our own selves and condemning others.

CXXI

ONE OF THE ELDERS had finished his baskets and had already put handles on them, when he heard his neighbour saying: What shall I do? The market is about to begin and I have nothing with which to make handles for my baskets. At once the elder went in and took off his handles, giving them to the brother with the words: Here, I don't need these, take them and put them on your baskets. Thus in his great charity he saw to it that his brother's work was finished while his own remained incomplete.

CXXII

ONE OF THE ELDERS SAID: Just as a bee, wherever she goes, makes honey, so a monk, wherever he goes, if he goes to do the will of God, can always produce the spiritual sweetness of good works.

CXXIII

ABBOT JOHN SAID: A monk must be like a man who, sitting under a tree, looks up and perceives all kinds of snakes and wild beasts running at him. Since he cannot fight them all, he climbs the tree and gets away from them. The monk, at all times, should do the same. When evil thoughts are aroused by the enemy, he should fly, by prayer, to the Lord, and he will be saved.

CXXIV

ABBOT MOSES SAID: A man who lives apart from other men is like a ripe grape. And a man who lives in the company of others is a sour grape.

CXXV

A GREAT NOBLE whom nobody knew came to Scete bringing with him gold, and he asked the priest of that place to hand it out to the brethren. The priest said to him: The brethren don't need any of this. The nobleman insisted and would not take no for an answer; so he put the basket of gold down at the entrance to the church and said to the priest: Those who want some can help themselves. But no one touched any of the gold, and some did not even look at it. Then the elder said to the nobleman: The Lord has accepted your offering. Go, now, and give it to the poor.

CXXVI

ABBOT MATHOIS SAID: Better light work that takes a long time to finish than a hard job that is quickly done.

CXXVII

THE FATHERS USED TO SAY: If some temptation arises in the place where you dwell in the desert, do not leave that place in time of temptation. For if you leave it then, no matter where you go, you will find the same temptation waiting for you. But be patient until the temptation goes away, lest your departure scandalize others who dwell in the same place, and bring tribulation upon them.

CXXVIII

ABBOT ZENO, the disciple of Abbot Sylvanus, said: Do not dwell in a famous place, and do not become the disciple of a man with a great name. And do not lay any foundation when you build yourself a cell.

CXXIX

ONE OF THE ELDERS SAID: Either fly as far as you can from men, or else, laughing at the world and the men who are in it, make yourself a fool in many things.

CXXX

THEOPHILUS OF HOLY MEMORY, Bishop of Alexandria, journeyed to Scete, and the brethren coming together said to Abbot Pambo: Say a word or two to the Bishop, that his soul may be edified in this place. The elder replied: If he is not edified by my silence, there is no hope that he will be edified by my words.

CXXXI

ONE OF THE ELDERS SAID: A monk ought not to inquire how this one acts, or how that one lives. Questions like this take us away from prayer and draw us on to backbiting and chatter. There is nothing better than to keep silent.

CXXXII

Blessed Macarius said: This is the truth, if a monk regards contempt as praise, poverty as riches, and hunger as a feast, he will never die.

CXXXIII

Two brethren went to an elder who lived alone in Scete. And the first one said: Father, I have learned all of the Old and New Testaments by heart. The elder said to him: You have filled the air with words. The other one said: I have copied out the Old and New Testaments and have them in my cell. And to this one the elder replied: You have filled your window with parchment. But do you not know Him who said: The kingdom of God is not in words, but in power? And again, Not those who hear the Law will be justified before God but those who carry it out. They asked him, therefore, what was the way of salvation, and he said to them: The beginning of wisdom is the fear of the Lord, and humility with patience.

CXXXIV

THEY SAID OF A CERTAIN GREAT ELDER in Scete: Whenever the brethren were building a cell he came out with great joy, and laid the foundations, and did not go away until the cell was finished. Once, going out to build a cell, he was very sad indeed. The brethren said: Why are you sad, Father? He replied: My sons, Scete will be destroyed. For I saw a fire kindled in Scete, and the brethren went out with palm branches and put it out. Again the fire was kindled, and again they cut palm branches and put it out. But the third time it began to burn and filled the whole of Scete, and could not be extinguished. That is why I am sorrowful and sad.

CXXXV

Abbot Hor said to his disciple: Take care that you never bring into this cell the words of another.

CXXXVI

ABBOT MOSES SAID: A man ought to be like a dead man with his companion, for to die to one's friend is to cease to judge him in anything.

CXXXVII

Certain of the brethren said to Abbot Anthony: We would like you to tell us some word, by which we may be saved. Then the elder said: You have heard the Scriptures, they ought to be enough for you. But they said: We want to hear something also from you, Father. The elder answered them: You have heard the Lord say: If a man strikes you on the left cheek, show him also the other one. They said to him: This we cannot do. He said to them: If you can't turn the other cheek, at least take it patiently on one of them. They replied: We can't do that either. He said: If you cannot even do that, at least do not go striking others more than you would want them to strike you. They said: We cannot do this either. Then the elder said to his disciple: Go cook up some food for these brethren, for they are very weak. Finally he said to them: If you cannot even do this, how can I help you? All I can do is pray.

CXXXVIII

AN ELDER SAID: A man who keeps death before his eyes will at all times overcome his cowardice.

CXXXIX

AN ELDER WAS ASKED by a certain soldier if God would forgive a sinner. And he said to him: Tell me, beloved, if your cloak is torn, will you throw it away? The soldier replied and said: No. I will mend it and put it back on. The elder said to him: If you take care of your cloak, will God not be merciful to His own image?

CXL

ONCE ABBOT SYLVANUS went away from his cell for a while, and his disciple Zachary with the other brethren moved back the garden fence and enlarged the garden. And when the elder came back and saw this he picked up his sheepskin and prepared to leave. But they fell at his feet and begged him to tell them why he was doing this. The elder said: I will not come into this cell until you move back the fence to where it was before. They did this immediately and he came in.

CXLI

ONCE TWO BRETHREN came to a certain elder whose custom it was not to eat every day. But when he saw the brethren he invited them with joy to dine with him, saying: Fasting has its reward, but he who eats out of charity fulfils two commandments, for he sets aside his own will and he refreshes his hungry brethren.

CXLII

THEY MADE A RULE in Scete that they would fast a whole week before celebrating Easter. But it happened that in that week some brethren came to Abbot Moses, from Egypt, and he cooked them a little vegetable stew. And when they saw the smoke coming up from his cell, the clerics of the church that is in Scete exclaimed: Look, there is Moses breaking the rule, and cooking food in his cell. When he comes up here we'll tell him a thing or two. But when the Sabbath came, the clerics saw the great holiness of Abbot Moses, and they said to him: O Abbot Moses, you have broken the commandment of men, but have strongly bound the commandment of God.

CXLIII

ONE OF THE ELDERS SAID: Pray attentively and you will soon straighten out your thoughts.

CXLIV

A CERTAIN BROTHER ASKED Abbot Pambo: Why do the devils prevent me from doing good to my neighbour? And the elder said to him: Don't talk like that. Is God a liar? Why don't you just admit that you do not want to be merciful? Didn't God say long ago: I have given you power to tread upon serpents and scorpions and on all the forces of the enemy? So why do you not stamp down the evil spirit?

CXLV

ABBOT PASTOR SAID: Do not dwell in a place where you see that others are envious of you, for you will not grow there.

CXLVI

Abbot Pastor said: If a man has done wrong and does not deny it, but says: I did wrong, do not rebuke him, because you will break the resolution of his soul. And if you tell him: Do not be sad, brother, but watch it in the future, you stir him up to change his life.

CXLVII

ABBOT HYPERICHIUS SAID: A monk who cannot hold his tongue when he is angry will not be able to control the passion of lust either.

CXLVIII

THE ARCHBISHOP THEOPHILUS, of holy memory, said, when he came to die: You are a happy man, Abbot Arsenius, for you have always kept this hour before your eyes.

CXLIX

W<small>HEN A CERTAIN MAN</small> had asked Abbot Agatho to accept a gift of money for his own use, the Father refused, saying: I have no need of it, since I live by the work of my hands. But when the other kept on offering the gift and said: At least take it for the needy, Agatho replied: That would shame me twice over, since I would receive money without being in need, and by giving away the money of another would be guilty of vanity.

CL

BLESSED MACARIUS told this story about himself, saying: When I was young and lived alone in my cell, they took me against my will and made me a cleric in the village. And since I did not wish to remain there, but fled to another village where a pious layman helped me out by selling my work, it happened that a certain young girl got herself in trouble and became pregnant. And when her parents asked her who was responsible for it, she said: That hermit of yours committed this crime. So out came her parents and seized me and hung pots around my neck and led me about along all the roads, beating me and insulting me, saying: This monk has raped our daughter. And when they had just about killed me with their sticks, one of the old men said to them: How long are you going to beat this foreign monk? But as he followed and tried to take care of me blushing with shame they insulted him also saying: What has he done, this man whom you are trying to defend? And the parents of the girl asserted: We will on no condition let him go unless the livelihood of the girl is provided for and unless someone will vouch for this man in case he absconds. So when I made a sign to the old man to do this, he offered a guarantee and took me away. So, returning to my cell, I gave him all the baskets I found, to sell and provide food for myself and my wife. And I said: Well, Macarius, now you've got yourself a wife, you will have to work harder in order to be able to feed her. So I worked day and night in order to make her a living. But when the poor thing's time was up, for several days she was tormented by labour pains and could not bring forth her child. And when she was asked about it she said: I pinned the crime on that hermit when he was innocent. For it was the young man next door who got me in this condition. Then he who had helped me, hearing this, was filled with joy and came to tell me all about it and to ask me to pardon them all. Hearing this, and fearing that people would come and bother me, I quickly made off and came to this place. Such was the cause of my coming to this part of the world.

NOTES

1. Salt was used to season dry bread.

2. "Lord have mercy on me a sinner." This is the basis for the "Prayer of Jesus," frequently repeated, and universally practised in Oriental monasticism.

3. Evagrius Ponticus, a great mystic, was also one of the most learned men in the desert and the prince of the Origenists at Scete. His treatise on prayer is a classic and has come down to us falsely ascribed to St. Nilus. The bearing of this "verbum" is not clear unless we realize that Evagrius probably had a lot to say when he first came to Scete.

SHAMBHALA LIBRARY

The Art of War: The Denma Translation,
by Sun Tzu. Translated by
the Denma Translation Group.

The Art of Worldly Wisdom, by Baltasar Gracián.

Backwoods and along the Seashore: Selections from
the Maine Woods *and* Cape Cod,
by Henry David Thoreau. Edited by Peter Turner

The Book of Five Rings, by Miyamoto Musashi.
Translated by Thomas Cleary.

The Book of Tea, by Kakuzo Okakura.

*The Erotic Spirit: An Anthology of Poems of
Sensuality, Love, and Longing,*
edited by Sam Hamill.

I Ching: The Book of Change, by Cheng Yi.
Translated by Thomas Cleary.

Love Poems from the Japanese, translated by
Kenneth Rexroth. Edited by Sam Hamill.

The Way of Chuang Tzu,
by Thomas Merton.

When Things Fall Apart: Heart Advice
for Difficult Times, by Pema Chödrön.

The Wisdom of the Desert: Sayings from the Desert
Fathers of the Fourth Century,
by Thomas Merton.